STILL
Standing

STILL *Standing*

DEALING *with* GRIEF, LOSS & SICKNESS

Reverend
YOLANDA MICHELLE
MURPHY

XULON ELITE

Xulon Press Elite
555 Winderley Pl, Suite 225
Maitland, FL 32751
407.339.4217
www.xulonpress.com

© 2024 by Reverend Yolanda Michelle

All rights reserved solely by the author. The author guarantees all contents are original and do not infringe upon the legal rights of any other person or work. No part of this book may be reproduced in any form without the permission of the author.

Due to the changing nature of the Internet, if there are any web addresses, links, or URLs included in this manuscript, these may have been altered and may no longer be accessible. The views and opinions shared in this book belong solely to the author and do not necessarily reflect those of the publisher. The publisher therefore disclaims responsibility for the views or opinions expressed within the work.

Unless otherwise indicated, Scripture quotations taken from the Holy Bible, New International Version (NIV). Copyright © 1973, 1978, 1984, 2011 by Biblica, Inc.™. Used by permission. All rights reserved.

Paperback ISBN-13: 9798868508639
Hard Cover ISBN-13: 9798868508646
Ebook ISBN-13: 9798868508653

Acknowledgments

I am grateful for the support, love, intellect, and time shared with me during the difficult times I faced. I am indebted to God as God is the keeper of my soul. I am indebted to my soulmate and husband Dale Lee Murphy for taking our marriage vows seriously. I am indebted to my Mom Mary Joyce Mason, siblings Lucious Lee Mason Jr., Alexas, Nicholas Mason, and Yvette for being there when the times were rough. I am indebted to my sons Kyri and Chase for taking such good care of their mommy. I am also indebted to my BFF Karen Johnson for shedding tears when I could not cry. I am indebted to my Women in Ministry colleagues for the many prayers that I felt each day. I am indebted to my Brothers in Ministry who consistently encouraged and poured into me. I give thanks for my for my family Sandra, Jack, and Brittany for pitching in to help with my sons. I also give thanks to my sister-in-law Barbara for sharing advice and experiences with me. Two special friends who took notes at oncology appointments, made sure I made it for chemo on time, and made sure I consumed healthy snacks and plenty of water.

I acknowledge the 2nd Episcopal District of the African Methodist Episcopal Church of the North Carolina Annual Conference. The dedication of both the Southern and Northern Districts, in making sure I took the time to rest and heal after every situation is immeasurable. I honor Bethel African Methodist

Episcopal Church in Currie, North Carolina, Myrtle Grove African Methodist Episcopal Church in Leland, North Carolina, and the church where I currently serve as pastor St. Mark African Methodist Church in Smithfield, North Carolina.

Introduction

I hold on to the promise of God: that God will never leave nor forsake me. The feeling of being overwhelmed can be quite extreme. Have you ever experienced yourself or witnessed another person go through so many trying situations that you wonder: *how is that person still standing? How is that person able to continue to get up every morning?* The years 2020 to 2023 were the most difficult years of my life. In those three years, I suffered two heartbreaking losses and battled sickness. Not to mention, I had a very demanding job and was in the middle of seminary. If there was ever a wrong time to go through a storm, 2020 to 2023 was it. But who am I to determine when storms should arise? One thing's for sure: I had to activate my faith and truly trust in the Lord.

Chapter 1

In March 2020, I remember being at St. Phillips African Methodist Episcopal Church in Wilmington, North Carolina for District Conference. My husband and I were in worship service and the choir began to sing, *He's Sweet I know* (Choir 1966). Now that I look back, the words of the song were so profound: "He's sweet I know, He's sweet I know. Storm clouds may rise, and strong winds may blow. I'll tell the world, wherever I may go I've found a Savior and He's sweet I know." As the tears streamed down my cheeks, I could envision my grandmother, Allie B. Mason, singing that very song. My grandmother had just passed away the previous August, at 103 years old.

As I was thinking about my grandmother, cell phones were buzzing all over the church. There was a virus that had hit the United States and was spreading very quickly. I worked for the federal government, and my supervisor had texted me that I would have to be screened for sickness before I would be allowed to work. She also informed me to pick up a paper decal to be shown in my vehicle. It was a time of uncertainty, and to be honest, it seemed unreal. Things moved very quickly—and then came the mask mandate. Everyone had to wear face masks covering their noses and mouths; you could not enter any business without one.

My son, Jack, had just begun working part-time. Jack was born with epilepsy but had the desire to become more independent since he had turned twenty-one years old. Because of his epilepsy, we had agreed that he would only work part-time. As the pandemic was getting worse, Jack was thrown into being a frontline worker stocking the essential items needed during the time of crisis. Jack's supervisors were calling him increasingly frequently to work and he would always say yes. I was concerned that Jack was stressed and lacking sleep. When confronted, he would say, "Mom, it will be okay. There are people who need me."

One night, as I was driving Jack to work, for some reason I asked him if God were to call him home, would he be ready? Jack replied, "I guess so." Jack had given his life to Christ at an early age, but I wanted to make sure he understood. I proceeded to tell him how God is a forgiving God, and no matter what he has done, all he has to do is repent of his sins. The Bible says: "Repent therefore and be converted, that your sins may be blotted out so that times of refreshing may come from the presence of the Lord, 'and that He may send Jesus Christ, who was preached to you before, whom heaven must receive until the times of restoration of all things, which God has spoken."[1] I continued to tell him to talk to God about it because I love him, and with the direction that this world is going, I wanted to make sure that we all go to heaven. Jack looked at me and said, "Yes, ma'am." I believe it was the Holy Spirit guiding me to share that teachable moment with my child.

I often brought up Jack's long hours at the store, but every time his supervisor called, he accepted. I was beyond worried. I heard a voice telling me Jack would not live beyond twenty-one years old. This was a still and quiet voice that I had been hearing for about two or three years. The first time I heard it, I immediately began to rebuke the devil. Because I was unsure of the message, I automatically assumed it was the work of the devil. The Bible says:

---

[1] Acts 3:19-21 (NIV)

"You may say to yourselves, 'How can we know when a message has not been spoken by the Lord?' Of what a prophet proclaims in the name of the Lord does not take place or come true, that is a message the Lord has not spoken. That prophet has spoken presumptuously, so do not be alarmed."[2] I had not shared it with anyone. I found myself constantly cautioning Jack, reminding him that his neurologist warned him of stressful situations and lack of sleep. Never could I have imagined what was about to happen. But wait a minute, hadn't I been hearing this voice saying Jack would not live beyond twenty-one and he was now twenty-one years old? Little did I know, God was preparing me for what was about to happen. I now know it was the voice of God speaking to me about my son.

---

[2] Deuteronomy 18:21-22 (NIV)

Chapter 2

On April 16, 2020, I was at work when I received a phone call from Jack at about twelve noon. He told me he wasn't feeling well. I replied, "Jack, you can't keep going like this with your condition. You must remind your supervisors that you have epilepsy, and you have to rest." I proceeded to tell him to go home, take his medication, and take a shower using my stress-relief eucalyptus wash. Jack said, "Mom, I didn't have a seizure, but I did tell my supervisor that I would not work tonight and need to take some days off to rest." I was relieved and satisfied with that answer. After work, I stopped by a furniture store and spoke with a salesperson. I then went home to begin preparing dinner for the family. My two younger sons were already home when I arrived. I asked my 14-year-old, Kyri, "Hey, where's Jack?" Kyri replied, "He just came in here about thirty minutes ago to check on us and said he was going to bed." I wanted Jack to rest, so I started dinner.

When dinner was almost ready, I told Kyri to wake his brother. Kyri hurried back and said, "Mom, I can't wake him!" I responded, "What do you mean, you can't wake him?!" I ran toward Jack's room, the hallway seeming to stretch unending before me, to find Jack motionless on his bed. I screamed and told Kyri to call 911. Being a nurse, I observed that Jack's lips and fingers were blue. I began CPR, as the dispatcher instructed me. I grew fatigued, so the dispatcher instructed Kyri to take over the compressions.

Something inside me knew that my beloved Jack was gone. I wanted to do everything I could to try to bring him back, so I switched with Kyri and started compressions again. Soon after, the paramedics came rushing into the room and said they would take it from there. The police officers tried to keep me calm as I hugged my younger sons sitting on the floor. I told Kyri to call my husband to inform him of what was happening. I then called my pastor to let him know and to ask for prayer. I knew that my child was gone, but the prayer was needed for strength.

You must know that when you go through moments of weakness, the Enemy is bound to try something. I suppose coworkers and church members had begun to hear of what was happening, because they started to show up at my home: two people with whom I had a good relationship, and one a not-so-good relationship. The reason the relationship was strained was because this person had done everything possible to try to discredit me. Not only that, but this person had also been known to mistreat Jack. The Bible says to love your enemies and pray for those who persecute you.[3] There was a lot of prayer going on regarding that relationship. Samantha was not in ministry, but we attended the same church. She had not visited my house before, as I am very particular about who enters my home. My home is my place of peace, and I wanted to keep it that way. I had no idea why she was there, but at the time, I was not concerned with who was there or why. It was like I was standing in a fog of unawareness.

Shortly thereafter, my husband walked through the door. The expression on his face was that of despair. As we hugged each other and cried, the paramedics came out of the room to tell us there was nothing they could do. I felt severe heartache; I couldn't catch my breath. I loved Jack with everything in me and now I

---

[3] Matthew 5:43-44 (NIV)

would never have another chance to hear his crazy laugh, to see his gorgeous smile, or to glimpse him in the mirror trying to ensure he had it all together because he was so fly. It was a pain that I literally felt in my heart. How was I supposed to function with my baby gone? As the paramedics went back into the room to gather their things, Samantha began gossiping about our pastor. It disturbed my spirit, but this was not the time nor place to confront her. The coroner arrived and did whatever it is that coroners do. Then, the paramedics and coroner came out of the room. The coroner informed me of what would happen in the days to come. The police officer gave me his card and informed me that, if there is anything he could do or if I had any questions, to contact him. The paramedic kneeled to me and told me he was so sorry, and I could go into the room and see my son. My husband and I, along with the others present, went into the room where Jack lay on the floor. I said goodbye. I prayed, and I gave him back to God.

After the coroner took Jack away on a stretcher, I knew I had the horrible task of calling my parents, my brothers, my in-laws, my aunt, and Jack's Godmother to let them know Jack had left us. It was one of the most difficult tasks of my life. I must have cried the entire night. The next day, I decided to call the person who was gossiping. She didn't answer the phone, but I left a message telling her it was wrong, and as a minister, I encouraged her to repent because life is too short. I never received a return phone call in response. As I prepared for Jack's funeral at my home church in Mississippi, I remember I continued to ask the Lord for strength.

Following Jack's funeral, I had moments of uncontrollable crying, though I would wait until no one was around. People would remark to me, "You are so strong!" But the truth is, I felt like I was crumbling. I threw myself into work and, one day, I had an epiphany. Jack's dream was to own his own T-shirt business.

He'd even given it a name: "Jack's Gifted Hands." I also knew that face masks were in such high demand. I have never sewn much of anything before, but I felt I would try it. I ordered a Cricut and a little sewing machine. I began making T-shirts and masks—and they were a hit! At the volume I was producing, I had a challenging time using the little sewing machine, so my mother suggested I invest in a better one, which I did. Once I replaced the machine, I was really moving masks and T-shirts, trying to keep myself busy. But with grief, no matter how much you try to distract yourself, the pain is still present. I lost myself in grieving for Jack: I had forgotten how to live. I had forgotten how to be present for my husband. I had forgotten how to be present for my other children. Amid my grief, I was appointed pastor at two churches. I knew these were daunting tasks, but I was willing to give God my all. I would get home from work and spend several hours on T-shirt and mask orders: I kept going and going until dark circles began to form under my eyes.

As 2020 waned into 2021, things began to slow down a bit. However, in January 2022, my sister-in-law called, frantic. My younger brother, Nick, had had an aortic dissection and was going into emergency heart surgery to have it repaired. With over twenty years of nursing experience, I knew that people who experienced aortic dissections usually bleed out in minutes; it is often fatal. I lost it. Nick and I are so close, only thirteen months between us. During our grammar school years, we both like cartoons and building club houses in the back yard. I thank God for his wife Yvette: she made sure I had a chance to speak with him before he was moved into the operating room. I was then faced with the challenging task of meeting my oldest brother Lucious Jr. and parents to take them back and forth to visit Nick in the hospital. My father took it extremely hard, as he could not bear to see any of his children suffer. As soon as he would enter the room, he would start to cry. I continued the back-and-forth between North Carolina and Virginia and prayed that everything would be alright. I remember asking God to not take Nick because it would be too much; with my heart, my spirit, and all that is within me, I trusted God to heal Nick.

Chapter 3

In February 2022, I had an appointment with my gynecologist. I reminded her that I was due for my annual mammogram, which she scheduled for March. When I arrived for the mammogram, I did not think it would be different from any other one: my previous results had all been normal, so for this one I expected a clean bill of health as well. During the procedure, the tech had a strange look on her face but did not say anything. So, I went home with no clue as to what was to come. A few days later, I received a letter in the mail stating that my mammogram was abnormal, and I would have to call and schedule a diagnostic mammogram and ultrasound. Even at that point, I was still thinking there was no way anything could be wrong. I went to have the diagnostic, and the tech said there were masses in my right and left breasts. Immediately afterward, I had the ultrasound. The tech then asked the radiologist to come in to review the results, and he explained that there was a mass in my right breast and a cyst in my left breast. I was scheduled for a biopsy.

When I went to have the biopsy, I remember asking God to please let the procedure be pain-free. I was afraid of pain, so I talked to my Heavenly Father about it. The moment I walked into the room where the biopsy would be performed, one of the two nurses present said, "We can see the fear on your face—don't worry, the doctor is very gentle. You won't have any pain." I felt relieved.

The doctor entered the room, but I knew the true Physician was already present. The biopsy did not hurt at all, and so I returned home to wait for the results.

I had been feeling like I was neglecting my family, so I decided to schedule a trip 11 days later to Gatlinburg, Tennessee. The children were out of school for spring break. My husband, our two boys, our granddaughter, and I left that morning April 18th for Gatlinburg. While driving, my phone received an email notification. It was a message from my doctor's online portal, "MyChart," entitled *Results*. I immediately opened the message and saw the words "invasive ductal carcinoma, lymphovascular invasion." With my nursing background, I knew that was a form of cancer. I looked at my husband, who has driving, and said quietly, "Babe, this email says I have cancer." I did not want the children to hear me. My husband replied, "Let's just wait until we talk to the doctor when we're back home." I could not comprehend what the email was saying. I performed my breast self-checks monthly and never felt anything. I had my yearly mammograms and had normal results.

My son had passed away, my brother had been in the hospital for four months, and now I discovered I had breast cancer through MyChart—*no one* should find out they have cancer through an automated message. I picked up my phone and called the hospital's breast navigator, who said, "The surgeon is on vacation, but someone should call you and explain the results." I never received a call. I had to endure the entire vacation with cancer on my mind. When we arrived at our cabin, I did another breast self-check and could feel the lump for the first time, which was the size of an egg. How could this lump suddenly appear?

The devil did his best to make me think this was the end. The devil continued to tell me to get my affairs in order because I was going to die. When I found myself alone in the cabin, I yelled to the devil, "I shall live and not die!" I shouted, "You will not back me into a corner!" Then I prayed and told the Lord that I trust Him with my life. I started to spiritually prepare for the fight. I had to ensure that I was mentally ready because I was being prodded into the fiery furnace, and I wanted Jesus to walk in there with me. I talked to the Lord, and I asked Him to take me through.

So, on that Monday after we returned from our trip, April 25, 2022, Kyri's sixteenth birthday, the day Nick was released from the hospital, I had my appointment with the surgeon. I went to that appointment with high expectations of what the Lord was going to do for me. I arrived with my husband and a good friend who was a nurse practitioner. I knew that my husband and I would not remember all the discussion points and so my friend was there to take notes. The surgeon walked in and introduced herself, and said she was quite angry at the fact that I had to endure an entire week without speaking to a medical professional about my results. The surgeon went on to explain that I did have breast cancer, but it was curable. The word 'curable' assured me that God was directing my path, and all I had to do was trust Him. My tears flowed as I praised God, right then and there. The surgeon said the cancer was at Stage II, and I would have to have surgery, chemotherapy, and possibly radiation therapy. I took a breath, looked the surgeon in her eyes, and said, "I'm ready to fight."

When we returned home, I hesitated telling Nick because he was recovering from his own traumatic event. However, after a time, he could sense that we were keeping something from him, and so I had to tell him I was diagnosed with breast cancer. My surgeon had reassured me that I was going to do well, and at the end of my appointment, had asked me to choose an oncologist as soon as possible. It was an easy task. I had worked for an oncologist in 2012, and his compassion and bedside manner were second to none. I immediately chose him as my doctor. God was moving and making a way. I knew God was walking with me. My surgeon had also said that she wanted me to have an MRI biopsy on my left breast, to make doubly sure that mass was a cyst and not cancerous. As I mentioned, I'm afraid of pain, but I realized that when we are going through the fire, there will of course be pain. I thought about Job in all his suffering. I know those sores had to be painful.[4] As Christians, we must realize that we will likely have to endure pain to reach our healing. I must admit, the MRI biopsy *was* painful. It was so painful that I couldn't control my tears—but Praise God, it was negative! I only had to contend with cancer in the right breast.

Two days later on April 27, 2022, I had my first my first oncology appointment with my friend. He told me he was happy to see me, but wished it were under better circumstances. He was patient and took the time to explain everything so that I understood the process. One important thing he mentioned was to consider taking a leave of absence from work. He reminded me that he has known me a long time, and I was always an over-achiever who wore multiple hats at my jobs. His concern forced me to examine myself and my practices. I had not stopped to enjoy life! I had not spent the time I should have with my family. I took his advice seriously: the next day, I packed up my desk at work and filed the necessary paperwork to take a leave.

Once my port was placed, I was scheduled to start chemo before any surgeries: I would receive chemotherapy treatments every three weeks. I have never been the type to worry about hair: I had sisterlocks (tiny dreadlocks) that were full, lengthy, and beautiful. My oncologist warned me that the chemotherapy would

---

[4] Job 2:7 (NIV)

cause my hair to begin to fall out starting about two weeks after my first treatment. My friend Evette would pick me up and take me to every appointment. She was so kind! Each time, she packed snacks and plenty of water for me. I was incredibly grateful for how she took care of me. Chemotherapy was tough, but God was a very present help. The side effects of chemo vary depending on the individual. I did not experience nausea, but I did have painful gastrointestinal issues. I began losing weight, but it did not bother me.

Around two weeks after my first treatment, I was sitting on the side of my bed running fingers through my sister locks. I looked down, and, as predicted, a handful was in my hands. I began to pull at the rest of the locks until they were all on the floor. I asked my husband if he could get the clippers and cut my hair. He looked at me a long moment and said, "I can't do it." I said, "I understand. I'll do it." So, I took the clippers and shaved off the rest of my hair and I did not look so bad bald. In fact, I thought I looked rather cute! Then something amazing happened: God showed up! After my first chemotherapy treatment, I could no longer feel the lump. I was so ready for my second chemotherapy treatment because I would always see a provider before the infusions.

At my next appointment, the physician assistant came into the room and reviewed my labs. Then he said, "Alright, Mrs. Murphy, I am going to perform a breast exam." He went about the task, feeling here and there for the lump I knew was gone. I said, "You can't find it, can you?" He replied, "I sure can't!" And went on to say how wonderful this was because it meant the treatment was working quickly. I never doubted God; I was able to witness God moving in my life. I was always tired and did not want to eat anything. I think it was God forcing me to slow down and rest. I was the one taking care of everybody and when my body started to fail, I was still expected to fix everything. My husband, Dale, stood beside me and took his marriage vows seriously.

When I was halfway through the chemo treatments, I had another visit with my surgeon and was informed that some of the cancer was microscopic and she was therefore unable to save my right breast. I immediately said, "Okay!" I knew that God had been with me every step of the way, and He would not leave me now. Shortly thereafter, I met with a cosmetic surgeon to decide if I wanted breast reconstruction. I asked, "Would it be better if I had both breasts removed?" He said, yes, it would be better in the way of reconstruction. He informed me that he would be in the operating room with my oncology surgeon. After the bilateral mastectomy, he would place expanders. The expanders would be filled with saline solution to stretch the skin in preparation for implants. In that moment, I felt that God was saying to remove both. I called the oncology surgeon's office and told the breast navigator that I had decided on a double mastectomy. I was told that I would need to have multiple surgeries. At the beginning of my healing journey, I would remark to Dale I would not have any surgeries. I had to remember the plans are not mine; rather, the plans for my life belong to the Lord.

Before the first surgery, I was not worried at all. I had given the entire situation to God and whatever His will, it would be perfect. When I awoke from anesthesia, Dale was still right by my side. I was feeling nauseated but wanted to drink something. The nurse brought me some water and I could not keep it down. Suddenly, I felt a pain where my right breast had been removed. The cosmetic surgeon came in and touched the area, which was very tender. He informed me I had to go back to the operating room because he believed I had formed a collection of blood, a hematoma. This time, I was given a patch to prevent nausea. Although I was drowsy, I remembered to call on the name of Jesus to go with me.

When I awoke the second time, there was no pain nor vomiting: I felt nothing except drowsiness from the anesthesia. I had to stay overnight but was able to go home the next day. Dale had taken a month leave of absence to help care for me while I recovered. God is such an awesome God! So much so that He sent people I call angels. I arrived home to a sea of pink flamingos in my yard that these angels had placed! Two of my colleagues from work were responsible for the surprise, as pink signifies breast cancer awareness. Nick and Yvette had driven down from Virginia and prepared homemade chicken noodle soup. Nick was making a miraculous recovery from the aortic tear, prepared a steak dinner for me. My neighbor sent over lasagna and salad for my family. Family members and coworkers sent money to order take out. In short, I never lacked anything because the Lord is my shepherd. I was still on leave from work, per my oncologist's recommendation, but there were always checks in the mail. God is Jehovah Jireh, for God provided for me when I was going through the fire.

Chapter 4

In January 2023, my oncologist informed me that he was preparing to retire. This news made me very emotional because I was afraid, he would be replaced with an oncologist who didn't care. Working as a nurse for almost twenty years, I'd crossed paths with providers who either took caring for their patients to heart or couldn't care less. However, my current oncologist wanted to prepare a plan before he retired, and I began to really listen. He told me that I would finish chemotherapy in June of that year, but he wanted me to talk with my gynecologist about having a total hysterectomy. I suspected this might be a problem because, in 2021, I was having severe pelvic pain, which led to the discovery that I had polycystic ovary syndrome (PCOS). I had to have my right ovary removed. It was at that time I felt I should ask her for a hysterectomy. She said no, and simply stated we should only remove the affected ovary. I explained how I was not a fan of surgery, so to ask my gynecologist for yet another operation was a big deal. My oncologist said the type of breast cancer I had was estrogen-positive, which meant having a hysterectomy would serve as a prophylaxis to lower the risk of the cancer resurfacing as uterine or cervical. My maternal aunt, Mamie, had survived her breast cancer but passed away when it came back as uterine cancer. So, I agreed that I would have this conversation with my gynecologist. He then said he would normally say I wouldn't need radiation, but he wanted me to see a radiation oncologist to let them make the determination. He took his phone out of his pocket and scrolled through his pictures showing me how his kids had grown. Finally, he showed me a picture of me. When I worked with him many years ago, he and his practice partner took us on a limo ride to Raleigh for dinner as a reward for working so hard. Of course, I balled at the photo because it signified to me that God knew these plans: God knew I would go through the fire, but He knew exactly who would be there with me on this journey!

The next week, I had an appointment with the radiation oncologist. My first impression of him was particularly good. He seemed compassionate and knowledgeable. He told me that, in his opinion, it would be best to have radiation to the affected breast only. His reasoning was, as the cancer was microscopic, the radiation would kill all remaining cancer cells. I had already begun getting my breast expanders filled by my cosmetic surgeon, so the radiation oncologist said I could not start radiation until the fills were complete. Meanwhile, Dale was planning a birthday party for me. I was so excited that it took my focus off what was coming and forced me to live in the moment. The party's theme was "Breast Cancer Warrior." The colors were pink, purple, and gold: pink for breast cancer awareness, purple has always been my favorite color, and gold for royalty, as I am God's daughter, the daughter of a King. The party was beautiful, and I was showered with love. My parents, my brothers and sisters-in-law, my best friend Karen, extended family, colleagues, sisters, and so many others showed up to celebrate with me. God was truly working to show me that I was enough. There were many times when I felt like I was pouring so much of myself into others, but no one was pouring into me.

Shortly after the party, I began radiation. I had to be in the clinic Monday through Friday, under the radiation beam for about fifteen minutes. I was extremely tired during and after radiation. It seemed like it would never end, so I had to regroup and ask God to give me the strength to get through it. I had twenty-eight rounds of radiation, and, near the end, I suffered severe burns to my right breast. The burns were very painful and, though I was strong throughout the whole ordeal, this was the point I felt my weakest. I would just lie in the bed and cry, but I still never questioned God. Who I am to not feel pain, to not endure the fire? I had to remember all the suffering Jesus endured on the cross. I had to remember that I had to 'go through to get through.' I had to remember that those who hope in the Lord shall renew their strength.[5] I had to wait for my healing, and while I waited, I praised God. I praised God for the good, the bad, and the ugly. I knew God had not brought me this far to leave me. It was at that point that I knew I had to push through.

In mid-April, my parents came to visit. My father wanted me to take care of myself, so he came to North Carolina to build me a garden. He planted seeds of tomatoes, watermelon, squash, green beans, and turnips. On the days I felt well enough to go outside, I would take Chase, my nine-year-old son, to help me pick the vegetables. My father had always been a provider for my two brothers and me. He was so hurt that Nick, and I were going through our respective ordeals. My mom was truly in denial that any of it was happening. She would call me and say, "You're fine, you're not sick." It hurt me deeply, because I craved for her not to think of me as the go-to person, the one who is always strong, the one who always held it together; I wanted her to know that I was not okay. However, I kept my feelings to myself and continued to walk through the fiery furnace.

---

[5] Isaiah 40:31 (NIV)

I scheduled an appointment with my gynecologist to discuss the hysterectomy. I entered the exam room wondering how the conversation would go. When she came in, she complimented me on my weight loss and my perseverance. I told her about the conversation I'd had with my oncologist, how he recommended a total hysterectomy. She said, "Well if you are not in any pain, a hysterectomy is not necessary." I explained to her that it should be my decision. I wanted to be heard. Numerous times, as a woman of color, I have felt unheard in health care. She reiterated that there was no medical reason I should have the surgery. I then said, in a stern voice, that my aunt had breast cancer that resurfaced as uterine cancer, and she passed away. My gynecologist had a shocked look on her face and replied, "Okay, we'll schedule you for surgery." I was scheduled for a total hysterectomy in May 2023, not because it was my body and my choice, but because I knew my family history. Two paternal aunts, my maternal aunt, Mamie, who passed away, another maternal aunt who was currently suffering from bladder cancer, and a first cousin were all breast cancer survivors.

I had the hysterectomy in May and felt weak and lethargic afterwards. I told Dale something was wrong. I called my gynecologist's office and asked for an appointment. Dale drove me to the office, but I had to walk in alone because of COVID restrictions. The gynecologist took one look at me and confirmed that something was indeed wrong. She ordered bloodwork and discovered I was severely anemic. She prescribed iron and vitamin C, and provided information to help raise my hemoglobin. The next month, I had my last chemotherapy treatment and rang the bell one last time. My family had filled the waiting room, and they applauded and showered me with hugs when I walked out. It felt amazing to be at what I thought was the end of this journey—little did I know, the journey would continue.

Chapter 5

Around this time, Nick and I had noticed that my father was losing weight. My mother scheduled him an appointment, and his primary care provider ordered a colonoscopy. The colonoscopy revealed two masses, and my father was scheduled for surgery to have them removed. When I spoke with him about it, he did not seem worried at all. If ever there was a man with strong faith, it was my father. Lucious Jr. and I stayed connected throughout the surgery. Afterward, the doctor confirmed he had removed both masses and there was no need for any chemotherapy or radiation. We were elated!

During his recovery, my dad wasn't eating much, and my mother was worried. I called him at the hospital and teased him about coming to Mississippi if he doesn't eat. He laughed and said he would try. On June 25, 2023, my dad asked my mom to come to the hospital. My mother gathered her things, and Lucious Jr. drove her there. All seemed well and Lucious Jr. left to return home. But then, my cell phone rang, and it was Lucious Jr. asking, "What does 'coded' mean?" I explained what it meant, and he informed me that my father's nurse had called saying dad coded and they were doing everything they could. I went into prayer, but I knew that God's will be done. Sometime later, Lucious Jr.'s fiancé Alexas, called me to say our dad had passed away. In that moment, everything stopped. I didn't want to accept that my father, my protector, and my provider had slipped away. I did not have a father anymore. I did not have anyone to call me 'Sugar' anymore. I used to spoil him with all the latest fishing gear, and, suddenly, I realized I couldn't surprise him with Amazon packages anymore. My family and I went to Mississippi in preparation for the funeral, and I had to write his obituary. My father's oldest sister and her daughter came to my mother's house to share stories, and as I listened to them speak, I really discovered how remarkable my dad was. I knew his love for God, but I didn't know all that he had been through at a young age. Though it may seem strange to some, writing his obituary was comforting to me. My father's passing was shocking, but I knew that my brothers and I had to continue his legacy. I'd suffered so much pain, but I was still standing.

As a pastor, I never quit giving and preaching the gospel. The congregation of one of the churches I pastored had just been allowed back into their sanctuary in August 2023 with the lifting of COVD precautions. I preached what I called my 'Sermon of Triumph,' and I'd like to share what I told the people on that day: "It's been a long three years. In fact, this is the first time I've stood in the pulpit and preached since I was appointed pastor. I have been preaching virtually, but it is good to stand before you. It has been a rough road, and it has been hard times. So, what happens when you are constantly going through trial after trial after trial? Hit after hit after hit? What do you do? Do you give up? Do you lay down? Or do you stand?

"I am reminded of Joseph, born to Rachel and Jacob, who was later called Israel. Joseph was the baby of the family, and we know how parents love the baby.[6] Joseph was loved by his father, Israel, more than any of his other sons. When those boys saw how much their father loved Joseph, they began to hate him. Joseph had a gift, a spiritual gift: he could interpret dreams. The very first dream that he told his brothers made them hate him even more. He explained the dream by telling his brothers, 'We were binding sheaves of grain out in the field when suddenly my sheaf rose and stood upright, while your sheaves gathered around mine and bowed down to it' Gen. 37:7 (NIV). His brothers were furious and did everything they could to get rid of him. They began to plot his demise but changed their minds and threw him into an empty cistern. However, before they did, they stripped him of his precious robe that their father had given him. If that wasn't enough, they sold him and pretended he was dead to his father. He was sold again. The Bible says the Lord was with Joseph and he prospered. Potiphar's wife lied about him because he turned downed her advances, and he was thrown

---

[6] Genesis 37:2-8 (NIV)

in prison again. But the Lord was with him. He used his spiritual gift of dream interpretation to get himself out of prison, and eventually he was elevated to overseeing Egypt.

"But Joseph never asked the question that we love to ask God when we encounter trials—why? Lord, why was there a pandemic? Lord, why did my child pass away? Lord, why did I have cancer? Lord, why do my friends hate me? Lord, why did my father pass away? Lord, why am I not popular? Lord, why can't I get that promotion? We have a problem when we ask God why. God does not owe any of us an explanation. Do you remember when you asked your parents why? Your parents would respond, "Because I said so!" I tell my children the same thing when they ask, 'why?'

"The Bible says: 'For I know the plans I have for you, plans to prosper you and not to harm you, plans to give you hope and a future' Jer. 29:11 (NIV). Joseph went through being thrown in a pit, to being sold, to being sold again, to being thrown in prison, to being an attendant of one of Pharaoh's officials, to overseeing Egypt. Sometimes you must endure A,B,C, and D to get to the E. You must survive the accusations, the battery, the chaos, and the devastation to get to the elevation.

"If God were to answer your why, it would probably go something like this:

"'Lord, why did my child pass away?'

"God would say, 'Well, you don't know what your child was going through each time they were sick. You don't know how much your child suffered in that car accident. See, for you to be motivated to finish the things you needed to finish and to climb the heights you needed to climb, your child is better off with Me.'

"'Lord, why did I have cancer?'

"God would say, 'Because to get through it, you had to go through it. I know you were sick but now you have a voice. You can tell others what you went through and how I brought you through the fire. You can witness My miracles because every morning you wake up and get out of bed, you're still standing.'

"'Lord, why do my friends hate me?'

"God would say, 'If they hate you, then they are not your friends. They are your enemies. They are in your life for a season. Hate can only motivate you. I told you to love your enemies, bless them that curse you, do good to them that hate you, and pray for them who despitefully use you and persecute you. Because through all the hate and the hurt you are still standing.'

"'Lord, why am I not popular?'

"God would say, 'Because you are seeking validation from people when you should be seeking validation from Me. You're looking for the wrong thing in the wrong place at the wrong time and from the wrong people. My Word says, "But seek ye first the Kingdom of God, and His righteousness; and all these things shall be added unto you." So, after you are finished being shoved back, criticized, lied to, and talked about, as long as you still believe at the end of the day, you're still standing.'

"'Lord, why didn't I get that promotion?'

"God would say, 'Because it wasn't in My plans for you to prosper that way. Because I have something better for you, if you would only trust Me and give yourself over to Me. Even though you didn't get that promotion, and you were passed over time after time, you're still standing.'

"'Lord, why did the pandemic occur?'

"God would say, 'Because I needed to isolate you so you can discover that God is bigger than the four walls of the church. That God is present in your house, in your living room, in your kitchen, on your telephone, on your computer. I needed you to realize that God can change the rules at any time, and I expect you to adapt. After the pandemic took so much, you're still standing.'"

Conclusion

I authored this book as a representation of the Most High God and to serve notice to the Enemy that I am still standing. The Enemy tried to do everything he could to destroy me. He did things that he thought would take me out, and it was difficult. I was knocked down so often. My family and friends would look at me sometimes in pity because they thought the enemy had won. Though I was knocked down and took many gut punches, I still trusted God. I went through the darkest valley and the shadow of death, but I feared no evil. God was with me. Because I trusted God during it all, I was like a tree planted by the waters, that spreadeth out her roots by the river. So, come what may, no matter how hot it was, my leaves are green, and I never ceased from yielding fruit. Thank God, I'm still standing.

www.ingramcontent.com/pod-product-compliance
Ingram Content Group UK Ltd.
Pitfield, Milton Keynes, MK11 3LW, UK
UKHW050204190225
455204UK00017B/154